HR APPROVED WAY TO SAY THINGS I CAN'T SAY OUT LOUD AT WORK

LEX BASIL

DEDICATION

To all the underpaid, over-caffeinated, and perpetually frustrated workers who manage to survive their 9-to-5 without snapping. This one's for you.

And to HR departments everywhere, may this book remind you of why I'm still employed (for now).

Work isn't perfect, but at least now you've got a weapon to navigate the battlefield with humor and grace. If you ever feel like you're teetering on the edge, just remember: there's always happy hour. Until then, keep your translations sharp, your sarcasm sharper, and may your emails always "find you well."
Happy surviving!

TABLE OF CONTENTS

THE OVER-EMAILER

What You Want To Say:

"DO YOU EVER SHUT THE HELL UP AND STOP SPAMMING MY INBOX?"

HR- Approved Translation:

"THANKS FOR THE UPDATE! I'LL REPLY DIRECTLY WHEN NEEDED."

THE USELESS MEETING

What You Want To Say:

"THIS COULD'VE BEEN A DAMN EMAIL, KAREN."

HR- Approved Translation:

"LET'S KEEP THIS BRIEF AND TO THE POINT."

THE OBNOXIOUS CO-WORKER

What You Want To Say:

"DO YOU ALWAYS HAVE TO BE SO LOUD AND FUCKING WRONG?"

HR- Approved Translation:

"GREAT ENTHUSIASM! LET'S EXPLORE THAT IDEA FURTHER."

THE MICROMANAGER

What You Want To Say:

"GET OFF MY DAMN BACK AND LET ME WORK!"

HR- Approved Translation:

"I'LL KEEP YOU UPDATED ON KEY MILESTONES."

THE PROCRASTINATOR

What You Want To Say:

"STILL WAITING ON THAT SH*T FROM TWO WEEKS AGO, GENIUS."

HR- Approved Translation:

"JUST FOLLOWING UP—ANY UPDATES?"

THE FEEDBACK GIVER

What You Want To Say:

"YOUR ADVICE IS ABOUT AS HELPFUL AS A FART IN A HURRICANE."

HR- Approved Translation:

"THANKS FOR THE FEEDBACK! I'LL KEEP IT IN MIND."

THE OVERSHARER

What You Want To Say:

"I DON'T GIVE A DAMN ABOUT YOUR DOG'S FUCKING HAIRCUT!"

HR- Approved Translation:

"THAT'S INTERESTING! LET'S REFOCUS ON THE TASK."

THE IDEA THIEF

What You Want To Say:

"WOW, STEALING MY SH*T AGAIN? ORIGINAL MUCH?"

HR- Approved Translation:

"I'M GLAD YOU FOUND MY SUGGESTION USEFUL!"

THE DISORGANIZED LEADER

What You Want To Say:

"THANKS FOR DUMPING THIS DUMPSTER FIRE ON ME WITH ZERO DIRECTION."

HR- Approved Translation:

"COULD YOU PROVIDE MORE DETAILS SO I CAN GET STARTED?"

THE CLUELESS QUESTIONER

> **What You Want To Say:**
>
> "ARE YOU F***ING KIDDING ME? I ALREADY TOLD YOU THREE TIMES!"

> **HR- Approved Translation:**
>
> "LET ME CLARIFY THIS FOR YOU AGAIN."

THE OVERACHIEVER

What You Want To Say:

"CONGRATS ON MAKING THE REST OF US LOOK LIKE LAZY SH*TS."

HR- Approved Translation:

"GREAT WORK! YOU'RE SETTING A HIGH BAR FOR ALL OF US."

THE LATE REPORTER

What You Want To Say:

"THANKS FOR TURNING THIS IN LATE, ASSHOLE."

HR- Approved Translation:

"I APPRECIATE YOU GETTING THIS OVER. LET'S AIM FOR EARLIER NEXT TIME."

THE MEETING DOMINATOR

What You Want To Say:

"DO YOU EVER SHUT THE FUCK UP AND LET SOMEONE ELSE SPEAK?"

HR- Approved Translation:

"LET'S HEAR FROM OTHERS BEFORE MOVING FORWARD."

THE OFFICE GOSSIP

What You Want To Say:

"STOP SPREADING YOUR BULLSHIT AROUND LIKE CONFETTI."

HR- Approved Translation:

"LET'S STICK TO THE FACTS AND FOCUS ON THE WORK."

THE BARE MINIMUM EMPLOYEE

What You Want To Say:

"WOW, CONGRATS ON DOING THE ABSOLUTE FUCKING LEAST!"

HR- Approved Translation:

"THANKS FOR YOUR CONTRIBUTION!"

THE COMPLAINER

What You Want To Say:

"ALL YOU DO IS BH AND MOAN. DO SOME FUCKING WORK!"

HR- Approved Translation:

"LET'S FOCUS ON SOLUTIONS RATHER THAN PROBLEMS."

THE OVERLY FRIENDLY BOSS

What You Want To Say:

"PLEASE STOP PRETENDING WE'RE BEST FUCKING FRIENDS."

HR- Approved Translation:

"THANKS FOR CHECKING IN —I APPRECIATE YOUR SUPPORT."

THE PERSON WHO DOESN'T READ EMAILS

What You Want To Say:

"TRY READING THE FUCKING EMAIL NEXT TIME, GENIUS."

HR- Approved Translation:

"PLEASE REFER TO MY PREVIOUS MESSAGE FOR DETAILS."

THE OVER-PROMISER

THE UNSOLICITED OPINION GIVER

What You Want To Say:

"LITERALLY NO ONE ASKED FOR YOUR DUMB FUCKING OPINION."

HR- Approved Translation:

"THANKS FOR SHARING! I'LL TAKE IT INTO CONSIDERATION."

THE CORPORATE SUCK-UP EXTRAORDINAIRE

What You Want To Say:

"YOUR LIPS MUST BE PERMANENTLY GLUED TO THE BOSS'S ASS BY NOW."

HR- Approved Translation:

"YOUR ENTHUSIASM FOR MANAGEMENT IS IMPRESSIVE!"

THE CHRONIC F-UP DELEGATOR

What You Want To Say:

"GREAT, NOW I GET TO CLEAN UP YOUR SH*T, AGAIN."

HR- Approved Translation:

"THANKS FOR FLAGGING THIS. I'LL TAKE IT FROM HERE."

THE MEMO MASQUERADING AS A MEETING

What You Want To Say:

"THANKS FOR WASTING AN HOUR OF MY LIFE FOR NO FUCKING REASON."

HR- Approved Translation:

"LET'S EXPLORE WAYS TO STREAMLINE COMMUNICATION IN THE FUTURE."

THE WANNABE BOSS WITH ZERO AUTHORITY

What You Want To Say:

"DID I MISS THE MEMO WHERE YOU GOT PROMOTED TO GOD?"

HR- Approved Translation:

"I APPRECIATE YOUR SUGGESTIONS, BUT I'LL TAKE IT FROM HERE."

THE WALKING, TALKING BAD IDEA MACHINE

What You Want To Say:

"WOW, THIS IDEA IS EVEN SH*TTIER THAN I EXPECTED."

HR- Approved Translation:

"THAT'S AN INTERESTING PERSPECTIVE. LET'S WORK ON IT A BIT MORE."

THE PART-TIME WORKER WITH FULL-TIME NERVE

What You Want To Say:

"CLOCKING OUT EARLY? GUESS THE REST OF US CAN PICK UP YOUR SLACK."

HR- Approved Translation:

"HAVE A GREAT EVENING! I'LL FOLLOW UP ON ANYTHING OUTSTANDING."

THE DEADLINE DODGER

What You Want To Say:

"DEADLINES? WHO NEEDS 'EM WHEN YOU'RE THIS LAZY?"

HR- Approved Translation:

"LET'S REVISIT THE TIMELINE TO ENSURE WE'RE ALIGNED."

THE GOSSIP-FIRST, WORK-NEVER EMPLOYEE

What You Want To Say:

DO YOU EVER WORK, OR JUST TALK SH*T?

HR- Approved Translation:

"LET'S FOCUS ON ACTIONABLE TASKS TO MOVE THIS FORWARD."

THE MAGICAL TASK TRANSFER ARTIST

What You Want To Say:

"HOW THE HELL DID THIS END UP ON MY PLATE?"

HR- Approved Translation:

"I'D APPRECIATE SOME CLARITY ON ROLES AND RESPONSIBILITIES HERE."

THE FONT CRIMINAL

What You Want To Say:

"IF I SEE COMIC SANS ONE MORE TIME, I'M GOING TO SCREAM."

HR- Approved Translation:

"LET'S EXPLORE SOME MORE PROFESSIONAL FONT OPTIONS."

THE HEAVY BREATHER IN THE OFFICE

What You Want To Say:

"WHY DO YOU SOUND LIKE A DAMN FREIGHT TRAIN?"

HR- Approved Translation:

"IS EVERYTHING OKAY? YOU SEEM A LITTLE TENSE TODAY."

THE PROFESSIONAL WINGER WHO FAKES IT ALL

What You Want To Say:

"WOW, YOU'RE WINGING IT HARDER THAN A DRUNK BIRD."

HR- Approved Translation:

"LET ME KNOW IF YOU NEED ANY SUPPORT OR GUIDANCE."

THE SHAMELESSLY USELESS OVERACHIEVER

THE PERPETUAL ANNOYANCE GENERATOR

What You Want To Say:

"WHATEVER YOU'RE DOING, STOP. RIGHT NOW."

HR- Approved Translation:

"LET'S CONSIDER A DIFFERENT APPROACH HERE."

THE MASTER OF UNREASONABLE REQUESTS

THE LIVING REASON FOR HAPPY HOUR

What You Want To Say:

"DEALING WITH YOU MAKES ME NEED A FUCKING DRINK."

HR- Approved Translation:

"I'M LOOKING FORWARD TO UNWINDING AFTER A PRODUCTIVE DAY."

THE BACKSTABBING BUS DRIVER

THE CREDIT-STEALING SUPERSTAR

What You Want To Say:

"STOP TAKING CREDIT FOR MY SH*T"

HR- Approved Translation:

"GLAD YOU FOUND MY CONTRIBUTIONS HELPFUL!"

THE ENERGY VAMPIRE IN RESIDENCE

What You Want To Say:

"THIS PLACE SUCKS THE LIFE OUT OF ME DAILY."

HR- Approved Translation:

"LOOKING FORWARD TO MAKING AN IMPACT EVERY DAY."

THE URGENCY ALARMIST

THE OVERENTHUSIASTIC GIF SPAMMER

What You Want To Say:

"I DON'T NEED A FUCKING DANCING CAT AT 9 AM."

HR- Approved Translation:

"THANKS FOR THE HUMOR! LET'S GET BACK TO THE AGENDA."

THE KID BRAGGER WHO WON'T SHUT UP

What You Want To Say:

"SHUT UP ABOUT YOUR KID'S FUCKING SPORTS ALREADY."

HR- Approved Translation:

"THAT'S GREAT! LET'S CATCH UP ON WORK AFTER."

THE ICEBREAKER ADDICT

> ## What You Want To Say:
>
> "IF I HAVE TO DO ONE MORE STUPID ICEBREAKER, I'LL LOSE IT."

> ## HR- Approved Translation:
>
> "LET'S SAVE TIME AND JUMP RIGHT INTO THE AGENDA."

THE INSTANT REGRET OF BEING AT WORK

What You Want To Say:

"COMING HERE WAS THE WORST DECISION OF MY FUCKING DAY."

HR- Approved Translation:

"LOOKING FORWARD TO A PRODUCTIVE DAY AHEAD!"

THE DAILY CLUSTERFUCK ENTHUSIAST

What You Want To Say:

"LOOKS LIKE WE'RE NECK-DEEP IN SH*T AGAIN."

HR- Approved Translation:

"LET'S TACKLE TODAY'S CHALLENGES HEAD-ON!"

THE HUMAN EQUIVALENT OF A PAPERWEIGHT

What You Want To Say:

"WOW, YOU'RE IMPRESSIVELY FUCKING USELESS."

HR- Approved Translation:

"LET'S COLLABORATE TO MAKE THIS MORE EFFECTIVE."

THE PAY GRADE EXPECTOR

What You Want To Say:

"I'M NOT PAID ENOUGH TO DEAL WITH THIS BULLSHIT."

HR- Approved Translation:

"I'LL ESCALATE THIS TO ENSURE PROPER HANDLING."

THE MORALE WRECKING BALL

What You Want To Say:

"CONGRATS ON BEING THE OFFICE'S BIGGEST PAIN IN THE ASS."

HR- Approved Translation:

"LET'S WORK ON FOSTERING A MORE POSITIVE ENVIRONMENT."

THE 'TEAM PLAYER' BULLSH+T PEDDLER

What You Want To Say:

"'TEAM PLAYER' IS JUST CORPORATE BULLSHIT FOR 'DO EVERYTHING.'"

HR- Approved Translation:

"I'M HAPPY TO COLLABORATE WHERE NEEDED!"

THE PROBLEM PUSHER EXTRAORDINAIRE

What You Want To Say:

"NOT MY CIRCUS, NOT MY FUCKING MONKEYS."

HR- Approved Translation:

"LET'S CLARIFY OWNERSHIP OF THIS TASK."

www.ingramcontent.com/pod-product-compliance
Lightning Source LLC
Chambersburg PA
CBHW051706250726